QUINOA REC

Easy Quinoa Recipes F
Lunch, Dinner, and ᴊ ᴖᴖᴖᴗᴦᴛ

One of my favorite memories with a friend of mine has to do with quinoa. My friend and I were starting to explore new healthy foods. We were joking around with each other one day and I mentioned that she should purchase some quinoa. She laughed, because she thought I had made up a new word to joke around with her. After looking at my face, she could tell I wasn't joking. Intrigued, she went online, googled quinoa, and hasn't looked back since.

Quinoa has become an integral part of my daily diet because of its highly nutritious value and it tastes great! I usually have it 3-5 times a week. Having grown up on pasta, my body was used to eating empty carbs. Quinoa was a game changer for me.

I wanted to write this book to introduce quinoa to you. Not only introduce it and explain its many health benefits, but also provide a comprehensive cookbook with some of my favorite quinoa recipes that I consume year round.

I hope you enjoy.

Copyright Fresh Publications 2014

Disclaimer

Table of Contents

Background on Quinoa

Quinoa, or "mother grain," can be traced back to its origin in the Andes Mountains. Inhabitants of Peru, Bolivia, Ecuador, and Chile have been consuming quinoa for over 5000 years.

The past few years have seen a strong rise in consumption of quinoa in the Western World, coming so far as having 2013 being named "The International Year of the Quinoa." It was recognized that not only does quinoa have a high nutritional value, but also plays a hugely important role in food security all across the world. Less developed countries are able to consume quinoa and also earn a living from harvesting it.

Even though quinoa is known as the "mother grain" and is consumed in similar fashion to wheat, oats, rye, and barley (all cereal grasses), it is not in the same biological family. In fact, quinoa belongs to the same family as spinach and beets. This is due to quinoa being a "pseudo cereal" because it is not a grass, but can still be used as flour by grounding it down.

Quinoa can grow in a variety of different conditions: sandy heavy soil, hot sun, slight rainfall, high altitudes, and below freezing temperatures. Not only this but every part of the plant can be consumed: the seeds, like you buy in the store, but can also be ground into flour, the leaves, and the stems.

Health Benefits

Now that we have discussed some of the finer logistical points of quinoa, I want to get into the good stuff....why it is so good for us!

Quinoa has many health benefits, which is the biggest reason it has gained huge popularity over the past decade.

As discussed above, quinoa is similar to grains like wheat and rye, but it surpasses these grains in its nutritional value. Grains like wheat and rye, have very low or inadequate protein levels, due to their lack of lysine and isoleucine. These two amino acids are missing in grains and are known as "limiting amino acids." Not having these two amino acids results in grains not being considered a full protein source. On the other hand, quinoa has a large amount of both of these amino acids, and thus is considered a full source of protein.

Quinoa's fat content is also better than grains. 63 calories of quinoa equates to 1 gram of fat, whereas 350 calories of wheat equates to 1 gram of fat. This fat includes essential fatty acids and mono saturated (heart healthy) fats.

Vitamin E is somewhat of a similar playing field for quinoa and grains. Neither contains high levels of vitamin E. However, quinoa does contain high amounts of tocopherols. Tocopherols are in the same family as vitamin E, and not found in most grains. A benefit of this tocopherol in quinoa is it's anti-inflammatory nature.

Finally, quinoa is found to have high phytonutrient and antioxidant benefits, which again separates it from grains. Antioxidants such as ferulic, coumaric, vanillic, and hydroxybenzoic acids are all found in quinoa. Some antioxidants are even more plentiful in quinoa than berries!

Preparing Quinoa

Due to the commercial processing methods, quinoa is not as bitter as it would be if found in nature. However, there is still some bitterness due to the outer coating of the seeds. To remove this bitterness, place the quinoa seeds in a strainer and run cold water over them. As you are doing this scrub the quinoa with your hands and taste to see if bitterness is still there.

Quick Cooking Overview

Throughout the remainder of this book you will come across many recipes that have a very similar first step. This is the process of cooking the quinoa. I want to go over it here just to give a simple instruction.

For every one part quinoa, you are going to cook with two parts liquid. For example if you want to cook 1 cup of quinoa, you are going to do so with 2 cups of water. Again, some of the liquids will change in this cookbook, this is to serve as a general guideline.

Traditional Directions:

Add the quinoa and liquid to a pot/saucepan
and bring to a boil. Once boiling, lower heat to
a simmer and cover. Let this simmer for 15-20
minutes, until all liquid is absorbed. You will
see that quinoa has become clear.

Dry Roasting Directions:

You can also dry roast quinoa before cooking if you desire a nuttier flavor. To do this place quinoa in a skillet over medium heat and whisk for about five minutes. After this step, finish cooking the quinoa the traditional way.

Quinoa Flour Directions:

We will also be using quinoa flour in some recipes. To create the four, you are going to dry out the quinoa by placing it in an oven at 375 F for 5 minutes. After 5 minutes, remove from oven and place in a blender where you pulse it until smooth. You then use this flour as your base for the recipe.

Now to the fun part!

Quinoa Breakfasts

Cherry Nut Quinoa

Ingredients:

½ cup quinoa
½ cup water
½ cup milk
½ cup dried cherries
½ cup cashews
1 tbsp honey
½ tsp cinnamon
½ tsp vanilla extract

Directions:

1. In pot, combine quinoa, water, milk, cinnamon, and vanilla extract and bring to a boil. Once boiling, lower heat to a simmer and let liquid absorb, 20-25 minutes.

2. When liquid is absorbed, remove the quinoa from the heat and mix in cherries, cashews, and honey until everything is well incorporated.

Morning Blueberry Quinoa

Ingredients:

½ cup quinoa
1 cups milk, nonfat
1 ½ tbsp maple syrup
½ lemon, zest
1 cup blueberries
2 tsp flax seed
Pinch of salt

Directions:

1. In pot, warm milk over medium heat. After 5 minutes, pour quinoa and pinch of salt into milk. Lower heat to a simmer for 20 minutes, until milk is absorbed.

2. Take pot off of heat. Mix in maple syrup and lemon zest and thoroughly combine into quinoa. As you are stirring everything together, mix in blueberries and flax seed.

Granny Smith Quinoa

Ingredients:

½ cup quinoa
1 Granny Smith apple
½ cup water
½ cup apple juice
1 tsp cinnamon

Directions:

1. Peel, core, and chop up apple into small pieces.

2. In pot, bring water and apple juice to a boil. Add quinoa and lower heat to a simmer. Let simmer for about 10 minutes and then mix in apple pieces. Continue stirring for another 10 or so minutes until all liquid is absorbed.

Prune Peanut Butter Quinoa

Ingredients:

½ cup quinoa
1 cup water
½ cup prunes, pitted and chopped
1 tbsp peanut butter
½ cup almond milk
¼ tsp ground cinnamon
Pinch of Salt
Pinch of Nutmeg

Directions:

1. In pot, bring water and salt to a boil. Add quinoa and lower heat to a simmer for about 10 minutes.

2. After 10 minutes mix in prunes, peanut butter, almond milk, nutmeg, and cinnamon.

3. Let simmer for another 5 minutes until all liquid is absorbed.

Greek Inspired Quinoa

Ingredients:

½ cup quinoa
1 cup milk
¼ cup almonds, chopped
½ tsp cinnamon
½ tsp salt
½ tsp vanilla
1 tbsp honey
1 dried date, pitted, minced
3 dried apricots, minced

Directions:

1. In skillet, toss chopped almonds over medium heat for 3-4 minutes, until golden.

2. In pot, mix together quinoa and cinnamon over medium heat until warm. Then add milk and salt and bring to a boil. Once boiling, lower heat to a simmer and cook until liquid is absorbed.

3. When liquid has been absorbed, mix in honey, vanilla, minced dates and apricots, and a portion of golden almonds. Combine thoroughly.

4. Toss remaining almonds on top of quinoa when eating.

Quinoa and Coconut

Ingredients:

½ cup quinoa
1 cup coconut milk
1 tsp coconut, shredded

Directions:

1. Combine all ingredients in a pot over medium heat. Bring to a boil, then lower heat to a simmer and let cook until all liquid has been absorbed.

2. Stir everything together thoroughly once cooked through.

3. Enjoy.

Wheat Free Quinoa Porridge

Ingredients:

½ cup quinoa
1 ½ cups almond milk
½ cup water
2 tbsp brown sugar
¼ tsp cinnamon
1 tsp vanilla
Pinch of Salt

Directions:

1. In pot, combine quinoa and cinnamon over medium heat. Cook for a couple of minutes, until warm, then add in milk, water, brown sugar, cinnamon, and vanilla and bring to a boil.

2. Once boiling, lower heat to a simmer and continue cooking until all liquid is absorbed. This should take 20-25 minutes.

Quinoa Pancakes

Ingredients:

1 cup whole wheat flour
½ cup quinoa flour
2 tsp baking powder
1 egg, beat
1 cup milk
1 tsp cinnamon, ground
Maple syrup

Directions:

1. Mix together whole wheat flour, quinoa flour, baking powder, and cinnamon in a large mixing bowl until well incorporated. Then mix in egg and milk and continue combining until everything is smooth and there are no air pockets in the batter.

2. Lightly coat a skillet over medium heat. Once warm, place a portion of the batter onto skillet. Let cook until top starts showing bubbles, then flip over and cook other side until it is cooked through. Do this for remaining batter.

3. Spread maple syrup over top to serve.

Quinoa Granola

Ingredients:

1 cup quinoa
1 tbsp maple syrup
1 tbsp olive oil
1 tsp cinnamon, ground
¼ cup flax seed

Directions:

1. Preheat oven to 350 F.

2. Lightly spray a baking sheet.

3. Rinse quinoa, and in a large bowl combine all of the ingredients. Make sure to mix everything together thoroughly so that quinoa and flax seed are properly covered with other ingredients. Lay mixture out flat onto the lightly coated baking sheet.

4. Place baking sheet in oven and let bake for about 15 minutes, or until color is golden. Mix it around every 5 minutes.

5. Let cool. This is best served over yogurt, cereal, or even as a snack by itself.

Quinoa Pumpkin Muffins

Ingredients:

¾ cup quinoa
1 cup pumpkin puree
¾ cup milk
¼ cup water
¼ cup whole wheat flour
¼ cup flaxseed meal
1 egg
1 tbsp chia seeds
1 tbsp cinnamon
½ tsp baking powder
1 tbsp honey
1 tbsp coconut oil
Pinch of salt

Directions:

1. Preheat oven to 375 F.

2. On a lightly coated baking sheet, spread quinoa and place into oven for 5 minutes, until it is slightly browned. Remove from oven and place into blender and blend until it becomes the consistency of a cornmeal.

3. Pour all ingredients into a large mixing bowl and mix together thoroughly. Once combined, let it sit for 20 minutes.

4. In muffin cup baking sheet pour batter into each cup until it is about ¾ full.

5. Place into oven and let bake for about 40 minutes, or until golden.

Banana Nut Quinoa

Ingredients:

1 tbsp quinoa
¼ cup water
¼ cup milk
½ banana, sliced
1 ½ tbsp oats
1 tbsp oat bran
1 tbsp walnuts, chopped
1 tsp brown sugar
¼ tsp vanilla
Pinch of cinnamon

Directions:

1. In pot, combine quinoa, milk, and water.
Bring to a boil, then lower heat to a simmer and
let cook here for about 5 minutes.

2. After 5 minutes, mix in banana, oats, and
cinnamon and continue to cook for another 5
minutes stirring often.

3. Once mixture reaches your desired
thickness, usually after those 10 minutes,
remove from heat and mix in chopped walnuts,
brown sugar, and vanilla.

4. Serve warm.

Quinoa Salads

Warmed Honey Salad

Ingredients:

1 cup quinoa
1 ¼ cup water
2 tbsp olive oil
2 tbsp red wine vinegar
1 tbsp honey
1 shallot, minced
½ tsp thyme, chopped
Salt and pepper to taste

Directions:

1. In pot, combine quinoa, water, and a pinch of salt and bring to a boil. Once boiling, lower heat and continue cooking until water is absorbed, will take about 15-20 minutes. Remove from heat and let cool.

2. While quinoa is cooking, take a separate bowl and combine olive oil, red wine vinegar, honey, minced shallot, and thyme. Make sure to combine everything thoroughly.

3. Mix quinoa with the honey mixture until everything is well incorporated.

4. Enjoy.

Pepper and Mint Salad

Ingredients:

1 cup quinoa
2 cups water
¼ cup olive oil
2 tbsp lime juice
¾ cup minced bell peppers
½ cucumber, peeled and diced
2 tbsp mint, minced
1 tbsp jalapeno, minced
1 scallion, minced
Salt and pepper to taste

Directions:

1. In pot, combine quinoa, water, and a pinch of salt and bring to a boil. Once boiling, lower heat and continue cooking until water is absorbed, will take about 15-20 minutes. Remove from heat and let cool.

2. In separate bowl, combine oil and fresh lime juice and mix thoroughly. Toss in the bell peppers, diced cucumber, mint, jalapeno, and scallions. Continue tossing and finally mix in quinoa.

Kumquat Salad

Ingredients:

1 1/3 cup quinoa
1 ½ cups water
2 kumquats
2 tbsp cilantro, chopped
¼ cup olive oil
2 ½ tbsp lemon juice
1 pear
1 cucumber
1 watercress, stemmed and chopped

Directions:

1. Peel pear and cucumber and chop into ½ inch cubes. Cut kumquats in half, remove seeds and chop into pieces.

2. In pot, combine quinoa, water, and a pinch of salt and bring to a boil. Once boiling, lower heat and continue cooking until water is absorbed, will take about 15-20 minutes. Remove from heat and let cool.

3. In mixing bowl, mix together kumquats, cilantro, olive oil, lemon juice and salt. Let this dressing sit for 10 minutes.

4. While dressing is soaking, take another bowl and mix together cooked quinoa, pear and cucumber cubes. When this is well mixed, sprinkle with the kumquat dressing and chopped watercress.

Artichoke Salad

Ingredients:

1 ½ cups black quinoa
3 artichokes
½ lemon
½ cup olive oil
¼ cup white wine vinegar
1 red bell pepper, diced
1 yellow bell pepper, diced
4-6 Boston lettuce leaves
Salt and water to taste

Directions:

1. In pot, combine quinoa, water, and a pinch of salt and bring to a boil. Once boiling, lower heat and continue cooking until water is absorbed, will take about 15-20 minutes. Remove from heat and let cool.

2. Take ½ lemon, and squeeze juice into a bowl of water. Take 1 artichoke and break off its outside leaves. After you break off the outside leaves, take a knife and cut off the remaining leaves, keeping only the bottom of the artichoke. Remove the stem and peel the bottom of the artichoke. Take a spoon and remove the choke. Finally take the remaining ½ lemon, rub it all over the artichoke bottom and place it into the lemon water. Do this with the other 2 artichokes.

3. Place the 3 artichoke bottoms in a pot of boiling water until they are tender, about 10 minutes. Drain them and then chop into ½ inch cubes.

4. Mix together olive oil, vinegar, and pinch of salt and pepper in a large bowl. Toss in quinoa, artichoke, and bell peppers.

5. Serve over lettuce leaves.

Carrot and Quinoa Salad

Ingredients:

1 cup quinoa
¼ cup pine nuts
2 carrots, cut in half long way and chop into half moon shape
3 tbsp olive oil
3 garlic cloves, minced
½ red onion, diced
2 tsp cumin, ground
1 tbsp sherry vinegar
2 tbsp mint leaves

Directions:

1. In pot, combine quinoa, water, a pinch of salt and bring to a boil. Once boiling, lower heat and continue cooking until water is absorbed, will take about 15-20 minutes. Remove from heat and let cool.

2. While quinoa is cooking, place pine nuts in a skillet over medium heat for a couple of minutes. When they become fragrant, remove them from heat and place aside.

3. Place olive oil in warmed skillet and sauté the onion and garlic until browned, should be around 5 minutes. Next, add in carrots and cumin and cook for an additional 5 minutes, until carrots become tender. Finally, mix in quinoa and sherry vinegar and combine everything thoroughly.

4. Garnish the salad with the pine nuts and mint leaves.

Tex-Mex Quinoa Salad

Ingredients:

1 cup quinoa
2 cups water
1 tsp cumin, ground
2 tbsp lime juice
6 tbsp vegetable oil
1 can black beans (15 oz.)
1 red bell pepper, diced
½ cup cilantro, diced
1 jar cocktail onions (3 oz.)
Pinch of salt and pepper

Directions:

1. In pot, combine quinoa, water, a pinch of salt and bring to a boil. Once boiling, lower heat and continue cooking until water is absorbed, will take about 15-20 minutes. Remove from heat, lay quinoa on a flat baking sheet, place in refrigerator for 20 minutes to cool down.

2. While quinoa is cooking and cooling, combine ground cumin, lime juice, and vegetable oil in a blender and pulse until well incorporated, creating a dressing. Taste with salt and pepper.

3. Combine quinoa, dressing, and all of the remaining ingredients into a large bowl and toss.

4. Enjoy.

Black Bean Quinoa Salad

Ingredients:

1 cup quinoa
1 can (15 oz.) black beans
3 tbsp sherry vinegar
1 tbsp soy sauce
1 tbsp lime juice
2 tbsp olive oil
6 scallions, white only, sliced thin
1 red onion, diced
1 red bell pepper, diced
¼ cup cilantro, chopped

Directions:

1. In pot, combine quinoa, water, a pinch of salt and bring to a boil. Once boiling, lower heat and continue cooking until water is absorbed, will take about 15-20 minutes. Remove from heat and let cool.

2. Meanwhile, create a dressing by combining sherry vinegar, soy sauce, and lime juice in a mixing bowl. Slowly add in olive oil while whisking. Mix in remaining ingredients until everything is well incorporated. Finally add quinoa and toss.

Citrus Bell Pepper Quinoa Salad

Ingredients:

2 cups quinoa
¼ cup and 1 tbsp olive oil
2 cups orange juice
2 cups water
1 red bell pepper
1 yellow bell pepper
½ cup pine nuts
1 tbsp white wine vinegar
1 tomato, diced
¼ cup basil, chopped
¼ cup mint, chopped
Pinch salt and pepper to taste

Directions:

1. In pot, heat 1 tbsp olive oil over medium heat. Mix in quinoa and let cook while stirring for about 5 minutes, or until it browns. Mix in orange juice, water a pinch of salt and bring to a boil. Once boiling, lower heat and let simmer for 15-20 minutes or until liquid is absorbed. Remove from heat and let cool.

2. While quinoa is cooking, take the red and yellow bell peppers and roast them on a grill until they are charred around their outside. Remove from grill, peel, seed, and then dice them into ¼ inch cubes. Place aside.

3. Take pine nuts and place them in skillet over medium heat for about 5 minutes, or until golden. Set these aside.

4. Finally, take a large mixing bowl, combine ¼ cup olive oil and white wine vinegar and whisk well. Toss in all the remaining ingredients, and make sure to incorporate everything thoroughly.

5. Enjoy.

Sweet Apple Salad

Ingredients:

1 ½ cups quinoa
½ cup olive oil
1 ½ lbs sweet potatoes, diced
¼ cup apple cider vinegar
2 Granny Smith apples, diced
½ cup parsley, chopped
½ red onion, sliced thin
8 cups baby spinach
Pinch salt and pepper

Directions:

1. Preheat oven to 400 F.

2. In pot, heat 1 tbsp olive oil over medium heat. Add quinoa, and stir for a few minutes. After 3-4 minutes, pour in 3 cups of water and bring to a boil. Once boiling, lower heat to simmer, and let cook for 15-20 minutes, until liquid is absorbed. Once absorbed, remove quinoa from heat and set aside.

3. While quinoa is cooking, take sweet potato cubes and toss with 1 tbsp of olive oil, salt, and pepper. When everything is well incorporated, place on a baking sheet and into oven. Cook for 25-30 minutes, until potatoes are browned and soft. Remove from oven.

4. Finally, take a large mixing bowl and combine remaining olive oil with the apple cider

vinegar. Whisk together efficiently, then add all remaining ingredients and toss until everything is well combined.

5. Enjoy.

Nutty Lemon Salad

Ingredients:

½ cup quinoa
1 cup water
½ tbsp pine nuts
2 tbsp cilantro, chopped
1 tbsp lemon juice
Salt to taste

Directions:

1. In pot, combine quinoa, water, a pinch of salt and bring to a boil. Once boiling, lower heat and continue cooking until water is absorbed, will take about 15-20 minutes. Remove from heat and let cool.

2. Toast the pine nuts in a skillet over medium heat for 4-5 minutes, until fragrant. Place in bowl and combine with all the remaining ingredients and toss well.

3. Add salt to taste, and enjoy.

Lunch and Dinner Meal Recipes

Cranberry Quinoa

Ingredients:

1 cup quinoa
2 cups water
1 tbsp olive oil
1 red onion, minced
1 cauliflower head, chopped up
½ cup cranberries
¼ cup fresh parsley
2 tbsp fresh lemon juice
1/3 cup toasted pine nuts

Directions:

1. Combine water and quinoa in pot over high heat and bring to a boil. Once it is boiling, lower heat and let simmer for 15 minutes, until water is absorbed.

2. While quinoa is simmering, heat the olive oil in a skillet over medium heat. Add onion and let cook until golden. Once onion is golden, add cauliflower and 1/3 cup of water. Cover skillet and let cook until cauliflower is tenderized.

3. When quinoa is finished cooking, combine it with the cauliflower in the skillet and then mix in the cranberries, parsley, and lemon juice.

Mix together thoroughly and then remove from heat.

4. Toss the pine nuts on top and serve warm.

Caribbean Quinoa

Ingredients:

1 cup quinoa
1 tbsp olive oil
½ cup red onion, minced
2 tsp ginger, grated
2 cloves garlic, minced
½ tsp thyme
¼ tsp each: cumin, allspice, coriander
1/8 tsp cayenne pepper
1 ½ cups black beans
1 pineapple, pitted and chopped
1 lime, using only fresh squeezed juice
2 tbsp cilantro, minced

Directions:

1. Add quinoa to water and bring to a boil. Once boiling, lower heat and let all water absorb, 20 to 30 minutes.

2. During the time quinoa is cooking, add oil to a skillet and place over medium heat. Add onion and bell pepper and sauté for 5 minutes. After 5 minutes, mix in ginger, garlic, thyme, cumin, allspice, coriander, and cayenne pepper. Continue stirring and cooking for another minute.

3. Add black beans and quinoa and continue stirring. Finally throw in pineapple pieces, lime juice, and cilantro and cook for a few more minutes, until everything is warm.

4. Serve warm.

Stuffed Peppers

Ingredients:

1 cup quinoa
2 cups water
2 bell peppers, large
1 onion, diced
½ lb mushrooms, diced
1 carrot, diced
¼ cup dried raisins
¼ cup sunflower seeds
1 tsp natural soy sauce, no preservatives added
1 cup tomato sauce, all natural
1 cup walnuts, chopped

Directions:

1. Add quinoa to 2 cups of water and bring to a boil. Once boiling, lower heat and continue cooking until all water is absorbed, about 20 minutes.

2. Meanwhile, Preheat Oven to 350 F.

3. While oven is heating and quinoa is cooking, remove the top of the peppers and the remaining flesh from around the stern.

4. Add 1 cup of water to a skillet and place over medium heat. Place onion in skillet and let cook until soft. Then add mushrooms, carrots, pepper tops, raisins, sunflower seeds, salt and pepper to taste, and soy sauce. Let

this mixture cook until everything is almost tender, about 5 minutes.

5. Once quinoa is finished cooking, add it to this vegetable mixture and mix together.

6. Lightly oil an oven baking dish and place peppers inside. Fill the peppers with the quinoa and vegetable mixture with any remaining mixture left around the peppers. Throw walnuts and tomato sauce on top.

7. Cover and place inside the oven. Let cook for about 30 minutes, until peppers are ready.

8. Enjoy.

Quinoa Sloppy Joe

Ingredients:

½ cup quinoa
1 tbsp olive oil
1 onion, minced
½ green bell pepper, minced
16 oz. can pinto beans
1 cup tomato sauce, natural
1 tomato, medium sized and diced
1 tbsp soy sauce, no preservatives added
1 tsp chili powder
1 tsp paprika
½ tsp oregano
¼ cup fresh cilantro, minced
Baby Spinach
Whole grain tortillas

Directions:

1. Place quinoa in a pot with 1 cup water and bring to a boil. Once boiling, lower heat and let cook for another 20 minutes or until water is absorbed.

2. Meantime, heat olive oil in a medium skillet. Add onion and cook until soft. Once soft add the minced bell pepper and continue cooking until each are golden.

3. Once the onion and pepper are golden, add the remaining ingredients: quinoa, pinto beans, tomato sauce, diced tomato, soy sauce, chili

powder, paprika, oregano, and cilantro. Let
this come to a simmer.

4. Continue cooking this over low-medium heat
for 5 minutes and continue stirring. Remove
from heat but continue stirring for another 5
minutes to make sure everything is well
incorporated.

5. Spoon into whole grain tortillas to enjoy.

Orange Quinoa

Ingredients:

1 ½ cups quinoa
1 tbsp olive oil
1 cup edamame
1 red bell pepper, medium sized, cut into thin strips
6 stalks bok choy, sliced thin
3 scallions, sliced thin
1 tsp sesame oil
3 tbsp soy sauce, no preservatives added
1 tsp ginger, grated
2 mandarin oranges, cut into 1 inch pieces
½ cup pecans, chopped

Directions:

1. Bring a pot that contains quinoa and 3 cups of water to a boil. Once boiling, lower heat and continue cooking until all water is absorbed, about 20 minutes.

2. During this time, heat olive oil in a skillet over medium heat. Place edamame and thin strips of red bell pepper in skillet and let cook for 3 minutes. Add bok choy, scallions and continue cooking for another couple of minutes, or until it is almost wilted.

3. Mix in quinoa and sesame oil and continue stirring thoroughly. While stirring, mix in soy sauce, grated ginger, and mandarin orange

pieces. Finally mix in chopped pecans. Cook until mixture is hot.

4. Serve warm.

Hummus and Quinoa Wraps

Ingredients:

½ cup cooked quinoa
¼ cup sun dried tomato strips
1 cup baby spinach
½ cup hummus, natural, no additives or
sweeteners
1 tomato, slice thin
2 whole wheat tortillas

Directions:

1. We will make one at a time.

2. Take one whole wheat wrap, flat on plate
and spread half the hummus throughout.

3. Next, place half the quinoa down the middle
of the tortilla and place baby spinach on one
side and diced tomatoes on the other.

4. Take sun dried tomato strips and place them
randomly.

5. Roll the tortilla up to secure all the
ingredients and enjoy!

Quinoa Turkey Meatloaf

Ingredients:

¼ cup quinoa
½ cup water
1 tsp olive oil
1 onion, diced
1 clove garlic, minced
1 lb ground turkey
1 tbsp tomato paste
1 tbsp tobacco
2 tbsp Worcestershire sauce
1 egg
2 tbsp brown sugar
Salt and pepper for taste

Directions:

1. Preheat oven to 350 F.

2. In pot, combine quinoa, water, a pinch of salt and bring to a boil. Once boiling, lower heat and continue cooking until water is absorbed, will take about 15-20 minutes. Remove from heat and let cool.

3. In skillet, heat oil over medium heat. Add diced onion and sauté for 5 minutes until it is softened. Mix in garlic and sauté for another couple of minutes. Remove from heat.

4. In a large mixing bowl, combine all of the remaining ingredients. Mix together very well, as it will be a moist mixture. In a loaf shaped

and aluminum foil lined baking sheet, spread
and shape the mixture.

5. Place in the oven for 45 minutes. After 45
minutes, check loaf to make sure there is no
pink in the center, or your thermometer reads
at least 160 F. Once it is cooked, remove from
oven, let cool for a few minutes and then enjoy.

South of the Border Quinoa

Ingredients:

1 cup quinoa
2 cups chicken broth, low sodium
1 tbsp olive oil
1 can (10 oz.) diced tomatoes
1 green chili pepper, seeded and diced
1 jalapeno pepper, seeded and diced
1 onion, diced
2 cloves garlic, minced
1 package (4 oz.) taco seasoning mix
¼ cup cilantro, chopped

Directions:

1. In large skillet, heat oil over medium heat. Mix in quinoa and onion and sauté until the onion becomes clear, about 5 minutes. Next, mix in the minced garlic and diced jalapeno and green chili peppers. Sauté for 2 more minutes.

2. Pour in remaining ingredients and combine everything thoroughly. Bring to a boil, then lower heat to a simmer for 15-20 minutes.

3. Garnish with cilantro and enjoy.

Shrimp Stir Fry

Ingredients:

1 cup quinoa
1 lb shrimp, peeled and deveined
1 ½ cups chicken broth, low sodium
2 tbsp olive oil
3 cloves garlic, minced
10 spears asparagus, trim, cut into 1 inch lengths
1 onion, diced
1 red bell pepper, diced
1 cup mushrooms, sliced
1 tbsp ginger root, minced
1 tbsp lemon juice
Salt and pepper to taste

Directions:

1. In pot, combine quinoa, chicken broth, a pinch of salt and bring to a boil. Once boiling, lower heat and continue cooking until water is absorbed, will take about 15-20 minutes. Remove from heat and let cool.

2. In skillet, heat oil over medium heat, sauté onion, garlic and red bell pepper for about 5 minutes, until onion is softened. Then, mix in asparagus lengths, mushrooms, and minced ginger root and continue cooking until asparagus is tender.

3. Once asparagus becomes tender, add shrimp and cook until they are pink and no longer clear.

4. Finally, add lemon juice and quinoa into mixture and toss until everything is thoroughly incorporated.

Peas and Quinoa

Ingredients:

1 cup quinoa
1 tbsp butter
2 cups chicken broth
¾ cup peas, frozen
¼ cup onion, chopped
1 clove garlic, minced
1 tsp thyme, chopped
½ cup romano cheese, grated
2 tbsp parsley, chopped
Salt and pepper to taste

Directions:

1. In a pot, place butter over medium heat and let melt. Add quinoa, and stir for a couple of minutes. Pour in broth, chopped onion, minced garlic, thyme, and pepper. Bring this concoction to a boil. When it starts boiling pour in frozen peas. Lower heat to a simmer and cook for 15-20 minutes until liquid is absorbed.

2. When quinoa has absorbed all liquid, stir in half romano cheese and parsley. Incorporate thoroughly. To serve, place in bowls and sprinkle remaining cheese on top.

Quinoa Casserole

Ingredients:

1 cup quinoa
2 cups water
1 tsp olive oil
2 cups broccoli, chopped
1 cup cheddar cheese, shredded
1 can (10 oz.) cream of mushroom
½ cup fried onions
½ cup sour cream
Salt and Pepper

Directions:

1. Preheat oven to 350 F.

2. In pot, combine quinoa, water, olive oil a pinch of salt and bring to a boil. Once boiling, lower heat and continue cooking until water is absorbed, will take about 15-20 minutes. Remove from heat.

3. Meanwhile, steam broccoli for a 5 minutes, until it becomes tender.

4. In large bowl, combine quinoa with the broccoli, cream of mushroom, cheese, fried onions , and sour cream. Add salt and pepper for taste, and mix together thoroughly. Pour this mixture into a greased baking dish.

5. Place in oven for 15 minutes, until it is browned.

6. Enjoy.

New Orleans Style Quinoa

Ingredients:

½ cup quinoa
1 cup chicken broth, low sodium
2 qts water
1 bunch kale, sliced
½ tsp creole seasoning
1 tsp olive oil
1 shallot, minced
Salt and Pepper to taste

Directions:

1. In pot, combine quinoa, chicken broth and a pinch of salt and bring to a boil. Once boiling, lower heat and continue cooking until water is absorbed, will take about 15-20 minutes. Remove from heat.

2. In separate pot, bring water to a boil and place kale inside. Cook for about 3 minutes, just until kale becomes tender. Drain, set kale aside.

3. In same pot, heat olive oil over medium heat, sauté minced shallot for about 5 minutes. Add in the tender kale and continue cooking until it reaches your desired preparedness.

4. Finally, mix quinoa into this kale mixture and sprinkle creole seasoning, along with salt and pepper to taste.

Soups and Stews

Quinoa Spinach Soup

Ingredients:

2/3 cup quinoa
2 16 oz. cans low sodium vegetable broth
1 tbsp olive oil
1 onion, diced
½ cup shredded carrots
2 cloves garlic, minced
1 can pink beans
2 tsp curry powder
1 tsp paprika
2 cups tomatoes, diced
6 oz. baby spinach
2 tbsp fresh parsley, minced

Directions:

1. In a large pot, place oil and heat. When hot, add onion and sauté until soft, then add carrots and garlic, until everything is golden.

2. After about 5 minutes, when everything is golden, add vegetable broth along with quinoa, beans, and remaining spices. Bring this to a boil and then lower heat and let simmer until quinoa is tender. This should take about 20 minutes.

3. When quinoa is tender, add in tomatoes and another 2 cups of water, and continue cooking for another 10 minutes.

4. Finally, add spinach and parsley and stir for another couple of minutes until spinach wilts.

5. Enjoy hot!

Vegetable Stew

Ingredients:

1 cup quinoa
2 cups water
1 ½ tbsp olive oil
2 medium potatoes, peeled, diced into ¾ inch cubes
2 cups butternut squash, peeled, diced into ¾ inch cubes
2 carrots, peeled, chopped
3 ripe tomatoes, diced
2 tsp ground cumin
½ tsp ground turmeric
16 oz. can chickpeas, no preservatives added
Salt and pepper to taste

Directions:

1. Bring 2 cups of water to a boil and add quinoa. Lower heat and let simmer for 20 minutes, until water is absorbed. Set aside.

2. Heat oil in pot over medium heat. Sauté onions until they are golden. Once golden, add potatoes, carrots, squash, and diced tomatoes. Just barely cover with water. Let this come to a simmer and then add all the spices, stirring them in. Cover the pot and let cook for 45-50 minutes, until vegetables are soft.

3. Mix in chickpeas and season with salt and pepper and continue cooking on low for another 15 minutes.

4. To serve, place portion of quinoa in bowl,
then pour stew mixture over the top and enjoy.

Chili

Ingredients:

1 cup quinoa
2 cups water
1 lb ground beef
1 can (28 oz.) crushed tomato
2 cans (20 oz.) black beans
1 green bell pepper, chopped
1 red bell pepper, chopped
1 tsp oregano
1 tsp parsley
1 tbsp olive oil
1 onion, diced
4 cloves garlic, minced
1 jalapeno pepper, seeded and minced
1 tbsp chili powder
1 tbsp ground cumin
¼ cup cilantro, chopped
Salt and pepper to taste

Directions:

1. In pot, combine quinoa, water, a pinch of salt and bring to a boil. Once boiling, lower heat and continue cooking until water is absorbed, will take about 15-20 minutes. Remove from heat and let cool.

2. In large skillet, sauté ground beef on medium heat until it is browned and cooked through. Set aside after draining any extra grease.

3. In pot, heat oil over medium heat. Sauté onion, garlic, and jalapeno for 5 minutes, until onion is softened. Mix in the chili powder and ground cumin and cook for another 2 minutes to let these spices incorporate themselves. Next add in the remaining ingredients except for the quinoa and ground beef. Cook for 20 minutes, until bell peppers are tender.

4. After the 20 minutes, mix in quinoa and ground beef. Let it come to a simmer while stirring for a few minutes.

5. Serve hot.

Lentil Soup

Ingredients:

½ cup quinoa
1 cup lentils
4 cups water
1 cup celery, chopped
½ cup carrots
1 tbsp chili powder
1 tbsp cumin
1 tbsp ginger, ground

Directions:

1. Simply combine all the ingredients into a large pot. Place over medium heat for about 45 minutes.

2. After 45 minutes, check vegetables to see if they have reached their desired tenderness. If not, keep over heat for another 15-20 minutes until they do.

Cannellini Soup

Ingredients:

1 lb dry cannellini beans
8 shiitake mushrooms, stemmed, sliced
½ cup quinoa
10 oz. spinach
2 tbsp canola oil
1 onion, sliced thin
2 tsp rosemary, dried
Salt and pepper to taste

Directions:

1. Cook cannellini beans by placing in a pot of water over high heat. Once water begins to boil, cover the pot, shut off heat and leave for one hour. Drain beans.

2. In a separate pot, pour 1 tbsp of oil over medium heat. Once warmed, pour in mushrooms and sauté for about 5 minutes. Remove from pot and set aside.

3. Pour in remaining tbsp. of oil in same pot and sauté onions for about 12-15 minutes, until they are caramelized. Once caramelized, add rosemary and beans and enough water to cover a little more than the mixture. Bring this to a boil, then lower heat and let simmer for 30 minutes.

4. After 30 minutes, toss in mushrooms and quinoa and continue cooking until quinoa

becomes tender, around 20 minutes. Remove from heat, add spinach leaves and stir until spinach wilts.

5. Enjoy.

Chicken Soup

Ingredients:

2 ½ cup rotisserie chicken, shredded white
meat, found in supermarket
1 cup quinoa
1 qt chicken broth, low sodium
3 cups water
1 tbsp olive oil
1 onion, sliced
3 stalks celery, chopped
2 cups carrots, chopped
1 tsp Cajun seasoning
1 cup quinoa
Salt and pepper

Directions:

1. In pot, heat oil over medium heat. Sauté
onion, celery, carrots, and Cajun seasoning for
about 5 minutes, until vegetables soften.

2. After those 5 minutes, add quinoa, chicken
broth, water, pinch of salt and pepper. Let this
come to a simmer before lowering heat. Cover
pot and let cook for a bout 15 minutes. After
15 minutes add the shredded chicken and stir
until everything is hot.

3. Spoon into bowls to serve.

Quinoa Desserts

Strawberry Pudding

Ingredients:

2 ¼ cup water
1 ½ cup rhubarb, chopped
1 cup strawberries, chopped
1/3 cup quinoa
½ tsp cinnamon, ground
½ cup sugar
1 tbsp sugar
½ tsp lemon zest, grated
1 tbsp cornstarch
1 cup greek yogurt, nonfat
1 tsp vanilla
Pinch of salt

Directions:

1. In pot, combine rhubarb, strawberries, quinoa, salt, cinnamon, and 2 cups of water. Bring this mixture to a boil, then reduce heat to a simmer. Cover the pot and let this simmer for about 25 minutes.

2. After 25 minutes, mix in ½ cup sugar and lemon zest.

3. In separate bowl, combine the cornstarch with the left over ¼ cup water. Whisk this together and then mix it into the pot with the quinoa and stir for another couple of minutes.

4. Take pot off of heat and let cool.

5. Finally, in small bowl, combine the yogurt, sugar, and vanilla mixing thoroughly.

6. To serve, pour pudding in bowls and top with the yogurt topping.

Cinnamon Sweet Quinoa

Ingredients:

½ cup quinoa
1 cup water
1/3 cup almond milk
1 cup strawberries
1 tsp vanilla
½ tsp cinnamon
¼ tsp cardamom
¼ cup chocolate chips

Directions:

1. In pot, combine quinoa, water, a pinch of salt and bring to a boil. Once boiling, lower heat and continue cooking until water is absorbed, will take about 15-20 minutes.

2. Once quinoa has completed cooking, pour in 1/3 cup almond milk as well as the strawberries, vanilla, cinnamon, and cardamom. Stir everything together while still on low heat for about 5 minutes.

3. Spoon into a bowl, sprinkle chocolate chips on top and enjoy.

Quinoa Lemon Pudding

Ingredients:

2 whole eggs
1 cup milk
2 tbsp lemon juice
2 tbsp lime juice
½ cup sugar
2 tbsp quinoa flour
½ tsp lemon zest
½ tsp lime zest
Pinch of salt
Ramekins (4 oz.) or muffin baking sheet

Directions:

1. Preheat oven to 325 F.

2. Break open eggs and split apart the yolks from the whites.

3. Combine the egg yolks with the milk, lemon and lime zests, and lemon and lime juices in a small bowl and whisk together.

4. In a separate bowl, combine the sugar, salt and quinoa flour. Combine the two ingredients in the two bowls together thoroughly.

5. Take the egg whites and whip them for a couple of minutes. Take a third and mix into the batter. Then, add the remaining amount, gently mixing it into the batter.

6. Grease the ramekins and pour batter into each one all the way to the top. Place ramekins into a baking dish, and then fill baking dish with hot water until it reaches half way up ramekins.

7. Place into oven for 25-30 minutes.

8. Enjoy warm.

Quinoa Chocolate Bars

Ingredients:

1/3 cup quinoa
2/3 cup water
12 dates, whole
½ cup almonds
1/3 cup coconut, grated
3 tsp water
¼ cup chocolate chips

Directions:

1. In pot, combine quinoa, water, a pinch of salt and bring to a boil. Once boiling, lower heat and continue cooking until water is absorbed, will take about 15-20 minutes. Remove from heat to let cool, then place in refrigerator for a couple of hours.

2. In a blender, place dates and pulse until they are well blended. Remove from blender and set aside. Next, do the same with the almonds, but make sure not to blend too thin.

3. Once almonds are minced, add the dates, coconut, and quinoa into the blender and pulse until everything is well incorporated. Remove from blender, place into mixing bowl, add a tsp of water at a time, until you are able to form a bar that stays together. Make as many bars as you can.

4. Finally, add chocolate chips to a skillet over low heat until chocolate is melted. Sprinkle chocolate on top of the bars and place in refrigerator until chocolate hardens.

Peanut Butter Banana Cupcakes

Ingredients:

For Cupcakes:

2 cups quinoa flour
2 tsp baking powder
½ tsp baking soda
½ tsp salt
2 tsp cinnamon
1 1/3 cup almond milk
3 ripe bananas, mashed
¼ cup almond milk yogurt (or any other)
1 tsp vanilla
½ tsp butter
1 tsp sugar

For Frosting:

1 cup peanut flour
½ cup sugar
½ cup almond milk

Directions:

Cupcakes:

Preheat oven to 350 F.

Lightly grease or line cupcake tray with paper liners.

Combine quinoa flour, baking powder, baking soda, salt, and cinnamon in a small bowl. Whisk together.

In separate bowl, thoroughly combine the almond milk, bananas, yogurt, sugar, vanilla, and butter.

Combine the ingredients from the two bowls, making sure everything is thoroughly combined. Once combined, spoon the batter into the cupcake tray. Place in oven and let bake for 20 minutes. After 20 minutes, or when done, remove tray and let cool.

Frosting:

Simply combine all of the ingredients in a bowl and mix together. Place into a bag, snip off a corner and drizzle onto the cupcakes.

Enjoy.

Quinoa Dessert Cake

Ingredients:

2 ½ cups cooked quinoa (about ¾ cup
uncooked quinoa)
1/3 cup almond butter
4 eggs
1/3 cup almond milk
1/3 cup maple syrup
1 tbsp cinnamon
1 tsp vanilla

Directions:

1. Preheat oven to 375 F.

2. Lightly grease an oven safe baking dish.

3. Combine the cooked quinoa with almond
butter in a small bowl.

4. In a separate bowl beat the eggs and then
mix in the almond milk, syrup, cinnamon, and
vanilla. Whisk everything thoroughly and then
add the quinoa.

5. Pour this into the pre-greased baking dish
and place in oven. Let bake for 30-35 minutes,
until it becomes golden. Remove from oven to
cool.

6. Enjoy.

Peanut Butter Chocolate Chip Cookies

Ingredients:

3 cups cooked quinoa (1 cup uncooked)
¼ cup coconut oil
½ cup maple syrup
¼ cup cocoa powder
½ cup peanut butter, creamy
½ tsp vanilla extract
¼ tsp salt
½ cup chocolate chips

Directions:

1. In small pot, whisk together coconut oil, maple syrup, and cocoa over medium heat. Let this come to a boil, then remove from heat. Add creamy peanut butter, vanilla extract and the salt and combine thoroughly. Finally, incorporate quinoa so that everything is well incorporated.

2. Lay parchment paper inside of a baking sheet.

3. Using a spoon, scoop out mixture and pour onto paper, keeping room between each. Once baking dish is full place it in refrigerator for about an hour, maybe more. Once cookies are firm, they are ready to enjoy!

Conclusion

Quinoa has changed my life. The recipes I included in this book are recipes that I have used the past few years. My hope is that you will incorporate these recipes into your daily diet. Take advantage of all the nutritional value quinoa has and let it help you lead a healthier life.

Printed in Germany
by Amazon Distribution
GmbH, Leipzig